The Portable
❧
Best Friend

Jenni—
    I thought you could
use a friend who's always
here when you need her,
can fit into your pocket,
and won't make a pass
at your husband.
             Love,
             Mandi

Sandy Weinstein

WITH CAROL WALLACE

The Portable

Best Friend

Wit and Wisdom to
Get You Through
Life's Rough Spots

WARNER BOOKS

A Time Warner Company

Copyright © 1996 by Sandy Weinstein
All rights reserved.
Warner Books, Inc., 1271 Avenue of the Americas,
New York, NY 10020

 A Time Warner Company

Printed in the United States of America
First Printing: March 1996
10 9 8 7 6 5 4 3 2 1

Library of Congress Cataloging-in-Publication Data

Weinstein, Sandy.
    The portable best friend : wit and wisdom to get you through
life's rough spots / Sandy Weinstein with Carol Wallace.
      p. cm.
    ISBN 0-446-67171-1 (trade)
    1. Conduct of life. I. Wallace, Carol. II. Title.
BJ1581.2.W38 1996
170'.44—dc20   95-39710
                                       CIP

Book design and composition by Giorgetta Bell McRee
Cover design by Karen Katz

For Elizabeth and Michael,
and Jeanette and Fil.
The wisest hearts I know.

Acknowledgments

Thanks to all our friends, portable and otherwise, who were never too busy to talk—and who have given and received enough advice to fill twenty volumes. And special thanks to our editor, Jamie Raab, whose patience, guidance, kindness, and enthusiasm made this project a delight.

Contents

Work Is Driving Me Crazy! 21

Life Is Driving Me Crazy!

(Big Worries, Little Worries, and Everything In Between) 39

Introduction

It happens all the time. I get good news, I reach for the phone. I get bad news, I reach for the phone. I worry about my job, my daughter, my new dining room chairs, and I start dialing. Within minutes of my call, the knot in my stomach loosens. And before long, I'm laughing, even howling, at the very thing that made me call in the first place.

Friends. If you're lucky enough to have even one really good one, you know what I'm talking about. She's the one who runs over with the rocky road ice cream every time your heart gets broken, and then agrees that he's a jerk. Who listens to the same old complaints, the same old troubles with your boss, and never says, "Enough already!" You can't imagine life without her, and you hope you'll never have to.

But friends aren't always there the moment you need them. Last week, these messages were on my machine:

Oh no! Where are you? I'm on my way to my job interview and I'm panicking. Are you there?
BEEP
Well, we finished unpacking. Now if I could just pack it up and move back home. It's so lonely here.
BEEP
I start the new job tomorrow. What should I tell myself to get through the first day? Call me.

They needed me, but I wasn't there. I know how bad that feels. Whether the problem is a major life event or another bad haircut, my heart sinks when I can't reach a friend for moral support.

Years ago, my friend Carol called in a panic. She was about to take an eight-week trip to Europe alone, and had a terrible last-minute case of the What-ifs: What if she lost her passport? What if she was held up by thugs on a night train to Paris? (At that time, our knowledge of Europe was pretty much limited to what we had seen in the movies.) The list went on. So I made her an audiotape she could play anytime, kind of like a one-sided version of our conversations. I tried to be reassuring while I touched on all the fears and situations I imagined Europe could produce. And while I can't remember a word of that tape, Carol claims it gave her the comfort and laughs she needed, just when she needed them. (Since Carol's memory is far better than mine, her recollections of those laughs, and our conversations over the years, helped me tremendously with this book.)

The *Portable Best Friend* (PBF) won't replace your best bud, but I hope it will give you comfort, reassurance, and laughs. And, unless you change purses, it will always be there when you need it.

So when it's three A.M. and you're worried about getting a job, or it's three P.M. and you're tearing your hair out with overload, turn to your *Portable Best Friend*. Look up the specific problem that's troubling you, or read about them all and see things you haven't even thought of worrying about. Out of the fifty in this book, you're bound to find what you need. The bottom line is, whether your troubles are big or small, the *Portable Best Friend* stands ready to serve.

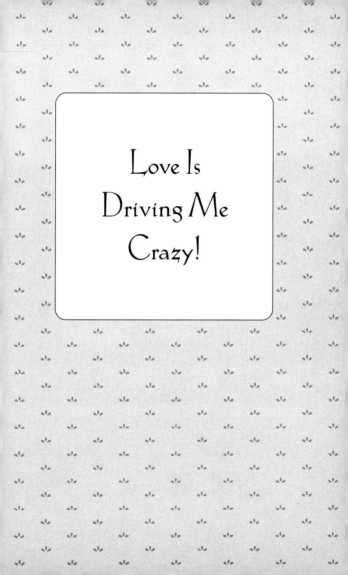

Love Is
Driving Me
Crazy!

Is He the One for Me?

I think he's it, but I've been wrong before. Can you ever be sure of these things?

PB4: Probably not. But you owe it to yourself to try.

1. Does your heart speed up when he walks in the room? Excellent sign. If, on the other hand, your stomach turns, keep looking.
2. Do you hope he never changes? Wonderful sign. If, on the other hand, you pray for a transformation, keep looking.
3. Have you seen him at his worst and not been repelled? Could you stand seeing it again and again? Good sign. If, on the other hand, one time was one time too many, keep looking.
4. Has he seen *you* at your worst and taken it well? Great sign. If, on the other hand, he bolted for the door, keep looking.

5. Do you look forward to his company, and then enjoy it when you have it? Terrific sign. If, on the other hand, you wonder what you were looking forward to, keep looking.

6. In the movie *Shenandoah*, Jimmy Stewart's future son-in-law asks for permission to marry Jimmy's daughter. The exchange goes something like this:

Do you like her? (Jimmy asks.)
I just told you I love her.
Yes, but do you *like* her? 'Cause if you don't, the nights can be long and cold, and contempt comes up with the morning sun.

You should listen to Jimmy. He makes a lot of sense.

Why Didn't He Call?

I pick up my phone every three minutes to see if it's working. I keep pressing the playback button on my answering machine even though it's not blinking. I was sure he'd call. Why hasn't he? I don't think I can stand it much longer.

PB4: Sure you can.

1. I bet he's been thinking of you; he's just so busy. You don't want a guy who's got nothing to do, do you?
2. He's probably afraid you'll blow him off, so he's trying to work up his nerve. You don't want a guy who takes you for granted, do you?
3. He may be ending another relationship— letting her down easy. You want a guy who's sensitive enough to do that, don't you?

4. Everyone knows a watched pot never boils. Get away from the phone. Now. That's when he'll call.
5. Okay, if worst comes to worst, and he really doesn't call, you've got to remember that a guy is like a bus: Even if you miss one, there'll be another one along in fifteen minutes.
6. Hey, who needs a guy who can't pick up the phone and call? Believe me, you can do better. And you will.

Getting Over Getting Dumped

What a jerk! And I thought this relationship was going somewhere. How could I be such a dope?

PB4: Please. *You're* not the dope here.

1. There isn't a person alive who hasn't been dumped. Anyone who denies it has a bad memory, or is a good liar. So take solace in the fact that your pain is universal.
2. If it's meant to be, it will be. He might not be able to live without you, and come crawling back. Of course, you might love living without him, and tell him to beat it when he does.
3. If he stays away, it really wasn't meant to be. Wouldn't you rather find out now? It's easier to handle a breakup than a crummy marriage or divorce. Cheaper, too.

4. You deserve a whole lot better—and better is out there somewhere. When you find it, you'll thank this guy for setting you free.

5. With any luck, you'll run into him in ten years. Not only will you look gorgeous, but you'll be surrounded by your beautiful husband and children. He will be alone and will have aged badly, proving once again that it is a just world.

6. Bottom line? This guy couldn't hold your coat. He's not half good enough for you. When you finally realize that, you'll want to sing about it.

Working Up to Good-Bye

I can't bring myself to tell him it's over, but I've got to end it. I need a transfusion of guts.

PBQ: Then start the intravenous.

1. Most guys don't threaten suicide or murder when they're dumped. Chances are, he'll just want his CDs back and ask if your roommate is dating anyone.
2. Relationships begin and end every day. It's the natural flow of things. You're just making sure things keep on flowing.
3. The actual scene is seldom as bad as the ones you've imagined. When you expect him to shout and beg, and he just says "Uh-huh, okay," you'll wish you'd done it sooner.

4. At this time tomorrow it will be over. Then you'll be free to dread something else.

5. What's the worst thing that can happen? Okay, but when's the last time the worst thing did happen?

Not Another Blind Date

It seemed like a good idea at the time. Now I'd give my Streisand tickets to get out of it. How am I going to get through this?

PB4: How? Easy.

1. Most blind dates are neither total bores nor serial killers. You may not see sparks, but you probably won't see bullets, either.
2. Remember that it's four or five hours out of your life; that's nothing. At least you're not having gum surgery or preparing your tax return.
3. Right now your date is probably as miserable as you are. That should make you feel a little better.

4. Amazingly enough, lots of people who meet on blind dates fall in love and get married. I've got a good feeling about this.

5. Even if the date feels like a tax audit, twenty-four hours from now it will be a bad memory, but a good blind date story.

6. It's only a date. You're not being asked to change the course of history, entertain the queen, interview for a job (but if you happen to be doing that too, see page 22), or perform open-heart surgery. All you have to do is sit through dinner and a movie. Do you know how many people would rather be *you* tonight?

Friends Are Driving Me Crazy!

Her Boyfriend Is Ruining Our Friendship!

Sure, it's her life, but why would she want to spend it with *him*? The guy's a loser. He'll make her miserable, and he'll ruin our friendship in the process. I'm having trouble keeping quiet.

PB4: Then buy a muzzle.

1. When Richard Gere married Cindy Crawford, everyone nodded in approval. When Julia Roberts married Lyle Lovett, everyone asked why. Who's to say what's right?
2. Maybe he has qualities you can't appreciate yet. Maybe in a year you'll wish he had a brother.

3. If they end up together, you can do what people have done for generations: Fake it. You think everyone likes their friends' husbands?

4. If she doesn't ask for your opinion, she probably doesn't want it, hard as that is for you to swallow.

5. Whatever you say about him will echo in her ears for years. Do you want to be the friend who dissed her husband?

6. If they break up, and she asks your opinion, anything goes. You can howl for hours.

Can We Really Travel Together?

I keep hearing horror stories about people who go away as friends and come back on separate planes. How can we avoid ugly arguments and bad feelings?

PB4: The only sure way is to stay home. But since you're going, realize there's an art to making it work.

1. Everybody has her own travel style. Remember that, when she wants guided tours and you want to wander freely. So compromise: Wander freely, and tell her all about it as you go.
2. Come on. If Arafat and Rabin could make peace, you two can certainly make it through a week together.

3. Hey, it's a vacation; lighten up. If you don't get worked up over little things, like missed trains and hotel rooms that can't hold you and your luggage at the same time, she probably won't either.
4. Okay, maybe you won't see every church in Rome because she sleeps too late. And maybe she doesn't get to every restaurant she wants to. You can always come back. With someone else.
5. So she snores, she's cheap, and she has to call her mother every day. Be thankful she's your traveling companion and not your spouse.
6. Come on, you're saving lots of money by splitting expenses. Isn't that worth a few jangled nerves?
7. Nothing is worth ruining a good friendship. Remember that *before* you call her stupid.

We're Drifting Apart

We just don't have much in common anymore. Can we get back on track? Or is this friendship over?

PB4: That depends.

1. Some friendships just fizzle out, but that doesn't mean you have to give them up completely. Have an occasional lunch. After all, you can probably talk to anybody for an hour, especially if you order wine.
2. Try to find common ground. But if you can't, try to find an excuse to go home. At least you tried.
3. If you can't even lunch with her, look at it as Survival of the Friendliest. Good friendships grow, bad ones don't, and there's nothing you can do about it. So lose the guilt.

4. Sure, everybody wants to be Lucy and Ethel, Mary and Rhoda, Laverne and Shirley. But look at the bright side: At least you're not Lenny and Squiggy, Eddy and Wally, or Thelma and Louise.

5. If you really feel bad about letting go, remember that "friend turnover" is a part of life. You grow and change; they grow and change. You go your own ways. Too bad you can't do the same with family.

Work Is
Driving Me
Crazy!

Interviews Make Me Nuts

I really want to impress them as the best candidate, not the most neurotic one. How can I get a grip so I get this job?

PBQ: Impress them? They'll be begging for you.

1. You've gotten to the interview stage, so you know they're impressed already. Now you just have to show them they're right. You're on a roll.
2. Of course you're nervous. They expect you to be. Did you know Lou Grant hired Mary Richards because she kept trying to hide the run in her stocking during her interview? He thought her nervousness showed she cared.
3. Good employees are hard to find. Remember that they need you as much as you need them—more, probably.

4. Remember that every interviewer was once on your side of the desk. Sure they have power now, but they're really not so different from your aunt Rose or your uncle Al. That should put the whole thing in perspective.

5. If all else fails, and you're completely intimidated, resort to the old trick of imagining them all in their underwear. It's worked for executives, singers, and Shakespearean actors; it can certainly work for you.

Why Would Anyone Hire Me?

I've been out of the workforce so long I've never even seen a fax machine. Who's going to hire a woman whose claim to fame is never having missed her turn to carpool?

PBQ: Whether you've been out of the loop, or never in it, give me a hundred applicants and I'll show you why you're better than ninety-nine of them.

1. Sure, working for years makes people experienced, but it also makes them tired and demoralized. Then you come along—eager to prove yourself and raring to go. You'd be a breath of fresh air for any boss!

2. Don't sell yourself short. You get more worthwhile experience in a day than lots of employees get in a month. From the time you wake up, you're managing, planning, expediting, and troubleshooting. Captains of industry should do so well.

3. You've had time to figure out who you are and where you want to go, and that will serve you well at any job. You think those young *pishers* out there can say the same?

4. Think about how many decisions you make every day and how many problems you handle at home. That's what you'll do at work. The only differences are that you'll wear panty hose and get paid.

5. My friend just went back to work as a lawyer after nine years and three kids. She was plenty nervous, until she saw that she gets more done in a day than the rest of them do in two. Compared to the stuff she crammed into every day for the past nine years, a job is a piece of cake.

Can I Do This Job?

I start my new job tomorrow, and I've got the dry heaves tonight. What if I'm a failure? What if they decide they hired the wrong person? What if they *did* hire the wrong person?

PB4: Failure, shmailure. This job has success written all over it.

1. You weren't hired as a favor. You got the job because you earned it. They think you're the best person for it. Whether or not you think you are really doesn't matter.

2. It's completely normal to get nervous. Don't you think President Clinton had his share of dry heaves before he was sworn in? You think Lee Iacocca never second-guessed himself?

3. Your self-doubts prove that you'll be good at your job. The incompetent ones usually think they can do anything.

4. No one ever does anything important on the first day. They're not going to ask you to submit your budget, make a presentation to the board, or lead the team in sales. Basically, you've just got to show up and look good.

5. What you need to do now is to lay out clothes that you feel great in. (Ideally, they'll be clean and pressed.) Take your mind off tomorrow with a good book or movie. Keep telling yourself how lucky they are to have you working for them. Think about all your past successes. By tomorrow morning, you'll feel so confident, you'll be asking for a raise.

How Could They Say That About My Work?

According to my boss, I've caused every problem but the national deficit. This wasn't the review I'd hoped for. How do I handle it?

PB4: With grace, of course.

1. First, bosses have to give you something to improve upon. Otherwise, it looks like you should be their boss.
2. Come on, you're focusing on every negative word you heard, and ignoring the good ones. Just do the opposite and see how much better you feel.
3. If the boss tells you you're perfect, you're going to ask for more money. They've got to dump all over you so you won't demand a raise.
4. It's not like you were fired or took a pay cut. Your life really hasn't changed at all.

5. Even the greatest captains of industry have at least one lousy review in their closets. They just don't tell anyone about it.

6. You think this schmo is the final word on talent? A different boss would think you were indispensable.

7. This falls into the "bag-it" theory. In other words, one bad review mixed in with a good performance record doesn't carry much weight. The powers that be see it, figure it's a fluke, and bag it. Many careers have been built on this principle.

Who Got the Promotion?

I work hard; I do a good job; and I was next in line for it. But they brought in someone else! Is that fair?

PBQ: No, but neither are short hemlines and bad legs.

1. Maybe they have something else in mind for you: a different promotion, or at least a healthy raise. There's no telling how the boss's mind works.
2. Think of all the corporate second-in-commands who have been passed over for the number one spot. When *they're* skipped over, the news makes gossip columns, business articles, and whispers in the corridors. At least *you're* not being smeared in public.

3. Some of your colleagues must think they deserved the promotion, too. There should be some comfort in knowing they're as miserable as you are.

4. This could just be a raw deal. Period. In that case, you have choices: You can live with it; you can find out why it happened and what's likely to happen in the future; or you can think about making a move. Once you make the choice, you'll be back in control.

5. There's always a chance the person who got the job will be bowled over by your talent, and lobby for your advancement. Wouldn't that be justice?

6. If Torvill and Dean were passed over for the gold, anything can happen.

Work with Her?!

Steve Erkel would be a better coworker. Roseanne would be easier to listen to. How can I work with her every day?

PBJ: The same way people have been working with each other for years.

1. When you work with her, pretend you're doing community service. You'll still be annoyed, but you'll feel better about it.
2. You can't be rude to her face, but you can make mental comebacks all day long. That will keep you smiling, and keep her in the dark. There's real comfort in that.
3. Look at this as a lesson in tolerance: If you can stand her, you can stand anything.

4. Imagine that you'll write a book someday and base a character on her. At least she'll seem useful.

5. If you've only got one coworker like her, consider yourself lucky. Most people are surrounded.

Uh-oh, I Blew It

I messed up big time at work. Now everyone is probably laughing at me. What an idiot!

PBJ: Stop beating yourself up and listen.

1. It's nature's law. Summer follows spring, night follows day, and people goof up at work, from shipping clerk to CEO. Today, it was your turn. Tomorrow, it's someone else's.

2. If you're *not* making mistakes, you're not making decisions. Sure, you can have a perfect record, but you probably won't do much along the way.

3. It's not the mistake that matters; it's how you handle it. If you tell the right people, and do what you can to fix it, no one will gripe. You've done more than most people do.

4. Forget the idea that everyone's laughing at you. Do you laugh when someone else goofs? Most people are just glad it wasn't them.

5. It's done; you've dealt with it; now forget it. Nothing's worse than someone who can't stop apologizing. That *will* make people laugh.

Fired! Me?

Stuff like this doesn't happen to me. It's humiliating, it's unfair, and I don't deserve it. I don't think *anyone* can make me feel better right now.

PB4: Oh yeah? Read on.

1. Getting fired is a little like not getting into the college you want. It happens for all kinds of reasons, which often have absolutely nothing to do with you. So lose the self-doubt and blame. Doubt and blame the fools who made the decision.
2. Lots of people say that getting fired was the best thing that ever happened to them. They reassessed, redirected, and eventually were happier than ever. A year from now you'll be singing the same tune. Give it time.

3. There's no shame in getting fired. It happens every day to all kinds of people. Anyone who thinks less of you for it probably doesn't watch *Seinfeld*.

4. When you not only bounce back, but exceed your wildest expectations, you can only hope that word gets back to the person who fired you.

5. What do they know, anyway? Michael Jordan was cut from his high school basketball team. Does that tell you something?

Life Is Driving Me Crazy!

(Big Worries, Little Worries, and Everything In Between)

Too Scared to Make a Change

I hate my job. My apartment depresses me. And I'm not so crazy about my boyfriend, either. I've got to make some changes, but I'm chicken.

PB4: Understandable. But chickens who stand still too long end up on the grill. Sometimes you've just got to fly.

1. Change is scary, but miserable ruts are scarier. When you weigh the two, doesn't the risk sound better than the rut?
2. Very few decisions are irrevocable. Even if you make a bad choice, you're smart enough to get yourself out of it.
3. Ask yourself: Could the next job be worse? The next apartment dumpier? The next boyfriend more obnoxious? Sure they could, but that's no reason to settle for what you don't want.

4. If Christopher Columbus hadn't been willing to make a change, we'd all be living in the Old World.

5. You don't have to change everything at once. It's like making the switch from whole milk to skim. Change overnight, and you'll hate it. But change to 2 percent, then 1 percent, then skim, and it's palatable. Remember that the goal is to improve your life, not to make yourself sick.

Hitting an All-time Low

My self-esteem has plummeted. I feel way too negative, even for me. Any way out?

PBQ: Loads of them.

1. First, don't be so hard on yourself all the time. You cut other people slack, do yourself the same favor.
2. Think about all the nice things people say to and about you. Take them seriously. Despite what you think, people don't make that stuff up.
3. My mother used to say that only idiots are happy all the time. Isn't it great to know that you're no idiot?

4. If you were half the loser you think you are, you wouldn't have such good friends who care so much. They don't like you out of charity, you know.

5. Is anything bad happening right now? See. That's something to be grateful for.

Too Busy to Have a Life

Women in commercials take bubble baths and lounge in the sun. I don't even sit down to eat. I'm sick and tired of being so busy.

PB4: Of course you are. It's time to kick back.

1. You need time for yourself as much as you need food and water. You shouldn't be any more hesitant to take it than you would be to eat an apple.
2. The nineties are fast. You can microwave food in seconds, fax documents in seconds, send E-mail in seconds. Since you don't plug into an outlet, no one should expect you to keep up the same pace.
3. You don't have to do everything everyone asks you to do. Start saying no, stop feeling guilty, and see how much more time you have.

4. You think big shots keep going without a break? They just delegate while they take it easy. If you can't be a delegator, at least refuse to be the delegatee.

5. Do you know one woman who takes bubble baths in the middle of the day? If you do, find out what she did to get there—and do it.

Time to Meet His Parents

In twenty minutes, I meet his parents for the first time. Should I be sweet and doting, or urbane and witty? My first impression has to be good, and I'm a wreck!

PB4: They'll thank their son for picking you.

1. Most in-laws want to like the person their child chooses to marry. It makes them feel like they've raised a child with good judgment. Imagine how good they'll feel about themselves when they meet you.
2. They want you to like them, too. That means they'll get to see their son and, eventually, their grandchildren. With that much at stake, you think they're going to give you a hard time?

3. Your fiancé has probably told them all kinds of wonderful things about you. Chances are they're thanking their lucky stars already. (And if he hasn't, you might ask him why not.)

4. They once had to meet their future in-laws, too. They expect you to be nervous, and are bound to be understanding.

5. First impressions don't count so much when you've got the rest of your life to get acquainted. Whatever happens tonight will just make a cute story to tell your kids.

Me Give a Speech?
Are You Nuts?

Are you kidding? A room full of people gathered to hear me speak? Just thinking about it makes my heart thump like Ricky Ricardo playing "Babaloo" on speed. Can I really do this?

PB4: Are *you* kidding? Absolutely.

1. If you can talk to a friend, you can do this. Just pretend that's what you're doing. The only difference is that they'll clap when you're done.
2. Hey, they don't ask schmos to speak. They asked you because you have something to offer. So all you have to do is tell them what they want to hear. You've been doing that all your life.

3. Remember that you're the only one who knows what you want to say. If you change it around or leave something out, no one will know or care.

4. So what if you pause, hesitate, and stumble? This isn't the Lincoln-Douglas debates (and who knows how many words *they* tripped over?). You're harder on yourself than anyone in that room could possibly be.

5. Besides, they'll be so happy it's you up there, and not them, that they won't care what you say.

6. Come on. You've *been* in the audience. You know that no matter how good the speaker is, your attention is divided between the speech and wondering when they're going to serve the sweet rolls. You think this audience is any different?

Buying Houses Is for Grown-ups

I've been over the numbers so many times my calculator needs a painkiller. Why do I feel like my real estate agent would sell me a bungalow on Three Mile Island and claim the location is ideal? Hey, this is harder than I thought.

PBQ: Yes, but it can be easier.

1. There are lots of houses out there, no matter how much your agent says, "You're making a big mistake if you let this one go." Maybe a house is a good deal, but you're the only one who knows if it's *right*.

2. My mother used to say that with houses and men, it's all a matter of chemistry. They either strike you right away, or they

don't. Of course she also said, "The difference is, with a house, you can always renovate."

3. People buy houses every day, and almost all of them get cold sweats in the middle of the night just like you do. It's a rite of passage.

4. Few people look at their prospective mortgages and say, "Wow, this is gonna be cheap!" Nausea is a perfectly appropriate response.

5. There really is nothing like the pride of ownership. Once the realtors and bankers are out of the picture, you'll feel like a million bucks. (Sure, you won't have that much, but you don't have it now, anyway.)

6. A few years from now the price you paid will probably seem cheap. Then you can pat yourself on the back for making such a smart investment, unload it for a profit, and start all over again.

But I Don't Want to Move

I don't know a soul; I didn't want to leave my home; and I can't find a good pizza to save my life. I'm lost here!

PB4: Not for long.

1. Of course you're overwhelmed. Moving is one of the highest ranked items on any stress meter. For now, if you unpack a couple of boxes *and* find a dry cleaner's, you're doing great.
2. Think of all your friends back home. They won't desert you, especially if they know you're miserable. So make sure they know, and get a place with a guest room.
3. Most cities have some charm and some kindred spirits. You'll find them when you least expect it.

4. Reach out. Talk to tellers, salesclerks, the Red Cross if you have to. You never know. It could lead to a new job, new friends, or at least free samples.

5. You'll find your own niche—friends, job, shops—that will make the new place livable. Once you find a good discount store, it'll make it perfect.

6. No one fits into a new place right away. A year from now, you could love it, or you could be on a plane out. But you don't have to decide today.

Living Alone

I'm sure I'll get used to it, but right now it's quieter and scarier than I like. If I can just get past the first few weeks, I'll be fine.

PB4: Fine? You'll flourish.

1. Think of all the people you know who live alone. They're not tougher or braver than you. Sure, some people may hate it, but some people hate chocolate shakes, too. You can't listen to the naysayers.
2. It's not like every killer, creep, and goof is headed for your door. There's no neon arrow pointing to your window, and they don't issue maps of your place to escaped cons. Don't talk yourself into a frenzy.
3. Think of all the time you'll have to do as you please. You can watch old sitcoms until dawn, read in peace, and eat where, when, what, and how you please.

4. You can fix the place up, or not, as you choose. No more roommate's photos of boyfriends or parents' Hummel figurines. Now you can make your own decorating mistakes.

5. You're free to walk around the place in any state of dress or undress you choose. No one will know whether you look like Madonna or Ma Kettle.

6. Once you have some friends over, it will seem more like home. Once they leave, you'll appreciate living alone.

Feeling Fat. For a Change.

I feel like a sausage that's packed too tight. I don't want to go out, I don't want to see anyone, and I sure don't want to try on last year's slacks. Can I get past this?

PBQ: Can tunics cover hips?

1. Except for supermodels and Olive Oyl, no one stays the same weight forever. It's not the end of the world. Just time for some temporary camouflage.
2. There's a seesaw rule for weight. You gain; your friend loses. You lose; your friend gains. It's nature's way of keeping you from getting smug when you're thin and depressed when you're not.
3. Forget supermodels. If more people could look like them, they wouldn't be

called super. Forget mannequins. They're made in factories, not in gene pools dripping with wide hips and flabby arms.

4. If you've been squeezing into tight clothes, no wonder you feel awful. Even the tiniest size fours don't look good if their clothes don't fit.

5. Sure, our obsession with fat comes from a society that puts too much emphasis on appearance. The trick is to find one that doesn't, and move there.

6. Thin is as thin does. And you do just fine.

I Blew My Diet and I Can't Get Back

I was doing great, but when I fell off the wagon, I fell hard. Now I'm beating myself up for it, and can't get my willpower back. Am I doomed?

PB4: Not even close.

1. Everybody splurges sometimes. It's like your body has a junk alarm set off by deprivation. It blasts; you dive in. It's not a sign of weakness—just proof that cheesecake is a necessary food group.
2. Don't replay the binge in your mind. It's history. Throw away the wrappers and move on.
3. You don't have to overcompensate by starving yourself. Just do whatever you were doing before your fall. Your guilt will disappear with that first turkey burger.

4. In the scheme of things, a few high-calorie, high-fat days don't mean a thing. It's the long term that counts, and you've got that nailed.

5. Look how good you are *between* junk alarms. Your self-control is inspiring.

Oh No! A Pool Party!

Will they let me in the pool with a coat? Or should I just give up and offer myself as a raft?

PB9: Nonsense. You'll have as much fun as everyone else.

1. Where is it written that you have to look like the rest of them? Hold your head up, toots. You've got plenty going for you.
2. And where is it written that you have to dress like the rest of them? Hold up your head, toots. Long flowing skirts are just as glamorous as bikinis.
3. Being thin is great for pool parties. But will it help anyone get a great job like yours? A terrific personality like yours? A sense of humor like yours? *Those* are qualities you can use year-round.

4. You show me the thinnest woman there, and I'll show you her overbite (or crow's feet, or flat hair). The point is, everyone's self-conscious about something.

5. Anyone can parade around a pool when she looks like a *Sports Illustrated* cover. Doing it when you're more ample takes guts and attitude, two qualities that will get you much further in life than thin thighs ever could.

Am I Indecisive?

I can't make decisions. Is that bad?

PB4: Only if you're an air traffic controller.

1. Being decisive is highly overrated. Look at the bad decisions people make every day. Lousy marriages, crummy jobs, ill-fitting suits. You're better off the way you are.
2. You're not indecisive, just cautious, which means that you'll probably never be swindled by a scam artist, or married to a bigamist. Does that sound so bad?
3. When it counts, you make decisions. And when you come down to it, how often does it really count?
4. You're in good company. Lots of great world leaders have been indecisive. If they weren't, we'd have been blown to bits years ago.

5. Next time you're in a group, notice who's making the snap decisions. You really want to be like that?

6. People who make snap decisions often make bad ones. People who take forever to make decisions often make bad ones. So what are you driving yourself crazy for?

I Stuck My Foot in My Mouth. Again.

Uh-oh. I wish I had kept my mouth shut. Will I ever learn to think before I talk?

PB4: What? And be the only one who does?

1. Hey, everybody puts their foot in their mouth now and then. Do the words "Dan Quayle" mean anything to you?

2. You don't have to be tactful all the time, just a lot of it. Because people forgive occasional slips from a tactful mensch faster than they forgive tactless slips from an occasional mensch.

3. If you feel your foot heading for your mouth, just do what Woody Allen's fading actress advised in *Bullets Over Broadway*. Don't speak.

4. Once you apologize for your faux pas, you'll probably be forgiven. Throw in a free lunch, and watch how fast it's forgotten.

5. Okay, so you put your foot in it. The only ones who never do that are dull people—and saints. Do you really want to be either of those?

Why Can't I Just Say No?

I know I'd look like a weasel, but I just don't want to (a) go to the movies with my girlfriend; (b) help my neighbor shop; (c) paint my cousin's apartment; (d) none of the above but something equally nauseating. Can I be a weasel and still be a nice person?

PB4: Sure. Some of the nicest people in the world are weasels.

1. You know how many people honor every commitment? About as many as eat just one potato chip. It just proves that you're human.
2. If you backed out of everything, you could be called a weasel. But one or two little shirks? Not even close.
3. There's backing out, and there's dropping the ball. When you don't show up to play the lead on opening night, that's weasel.

When you cancel a date with a friend, that's life.

4. Just the fact that you feel bad shows you're no weasel. Real weasels leave you hanging and never give it a second thought.

5. Next time, before you commit, try to remember that "No" is a complete sentence.

New Health Club, Same Old Body

They're going to wonder when the blimp landed. I want to work out, but do I have to do it with women who are the size of my purse? How do I get fit without feeling awful?

PB4: Awful? You'll feel better than ever.

1. It's a health club, not a nightclub. You're going there to exercise. Whether the other women look like Demi Moore, Mary Tyler Moore, or Dudley Moore is irrelevant.
2. Stop fixating on the skinny ones and look for the flabby ones. If there aren't any, shop for another health club.

3. Most women don't consider leotards their best look, but those who do invariably flaunt it at health clubs. Who cares? A pair of sweats makes a statement, too.

4. This isn't a pageant. So if they act like it's a swimsuit competition, ignore them. No matter how great they look, nobody's handing out tiaras.

5. You could look all dolled up, too. But you've got better sense than to waste a Saturday night look on a Wednesday night sweat session.

And I Thought My Last Cut Was Bad

HELP! My grandmother's hairdo looks good by comparison. This is the worst cut yet!

PB4: You think so now. But wait, there'll be worse. Don't let it throw you.

1. So, you went in with a picture of Claudia Schiffer and came out looking like Queen Elizabeth. At least now you know why she wears those dopey hats.
2. If the names Farrah, Carol Brady, or Kato have been used to describe your hair, it could be time for a new look. Or time to look for a new stylist.
3. A bad cut is like a stock market crisis. It's better to be patient than to panic. So fight the urge to cut your hair—or your wrists.

4. Keep telling yourself that bad cuts happen to good people. All the time. Why else would they have invented electric rollers, spray-on volume, and hair extensions?

5. Whatever you do, when you run into people you know, don't replace "Hi!" with "Can you believe this haircut?" Just because it's on your mind doesn't mean it's on everyone else's.

Addicted to Soaps and Ashamed

I pretend I don't know Erica Kane from Citizen Kane. But the truth is, I can name every husband she ever had. I worry about being a closet addict.

PB9: Forget it! Worry about something real, like Enchantment stock prices.

1. Hey, what's not to like? You get sex, power, and greed. Sure, you can get that on C-SPAN, too, but soaps give you better hairdo ideas.
2. Every day, you're whisked off to towns where people have homes you can only dream of and looks you'd only die for. Then you get to watch them pay for all that with problems that would only kill you. Who wouldn't get sucked in?

3. You know how crowded that closet you're in is? It's filled with politicians and CEOs who are as addicted as you are. Where do you think they get half their crazy ideas?

4. When Dickens started out, his writing was considered cheap entertainment for the masses. Which means that in a hundred years, soaps could be as classic as *A Tale of Two Cities*.

5. Soaps are educational. Where else can you learn the inner workings of a D.A.'s office, a crook's mind, and an adulterer's heart—while you do your dishes?

6. There's plenty of entertainment that's worse. Okay, there's plenty that's better, but at noon?

What's the Point of High School Reunions, Anyway?

I'm trying to make myself look twenty years younger, but it's not happening. Part of me wants to go, part of me wants to lose twenty pounds and have my eyes done, and part of me hopes that Sharon Zimmerman looks like dogmeat. What was I thinking when I paid for that chicken dinner?

PB4: You were probably curious, nostalgic, and masochistic. But if you're going, you might as well go in style.

1. Here's the good news: Kids who were incredibly cool, good-looking, and popular usually peak somewhere between study hall and college. Guys who once broke hearts walk into reunions bald, paunchy, and looking for a bankruptcy lawyer. So don't be intimidated by past glories. Just be glad you're not in this category. But if you are, keep your failures to yourself, and

be so nice to everyone that they'll think twice before they rip you up the back.

2. On the other hand, head-turners like Michelle Pfeiffer and Geena Davis weren't high school heartthrobs, just late bloomers. These types walk into reunions drop-dead gorgeous, talking about their multinational corporations. This proves it's a just world. If you're one of them, enjoy every minute of it.

3. You've got plenty going for you. Unless you're a celebrity, most of your classmates will only know what you tell them, anyway. So tell them about your lunch with Redford and the time you had dinner with Jackie O. Let them prove you didn't.

4. No matter how bad you think you look, don't act like you do. It's all in your head, anyhow.

5. No matter how good you think you look, don't act like you do. They'll look for faults.

6. Everyone in that room will be self-conscious. Tell them they look better than ever, and they'll be your friends for life.

When I Splurge I Feel Guilty

Other people buy themselves nice things. Dine in fine restaurants. Me? I spend more than $7.50, and I'm racked with guilt. Why can't I be more generous to myself?

PBQ: You can and you will.

1. There's a difference between buying a fancy dinner and buying a yacht. One can make you feel guilty; the other can make you feel gassy. Where's the guilt in that?
2. Hey, no one's telling you to break the bank on a Ferrari. But if a great sweater makes you happy, doesn't eat your rent money, and brings out your eyes, how bad can it be?
3. Don't worry that you'll splurge a few times and suddenly turn into Ivana Trump. She had years of practice and The Donald to bankroll her.

4. What's the worst that can happen? You lose your fear of price tags, and you start eating at restaurants that don't have drive-throughs. That's a good thing.

5. Chances are that if you spend the dough to get what you really want, you'll quickly forget all about the extra money it cost. If you don't, you'll always think about how great the coat, the meal, or the trip would have been.

Shakespeare Was Right. Don't Borrow.

My friend trusted me with her beloved cashmere blazer, and I turned it into a tablecloth from *Animal House*. Don't tell me to replace it—she bought it in Paris. Can this friendship be saved?

PBQ: Why not?

1. Look, anyone can spill wine or sit on a brownie. You think the friend who loaned it to you never looked like she used a dribble glass?
2. There are experts who can fix anything. Don't panic until you've tried most of them. Your efforts will impress her so much, she'll forget how mad she is.

3. Deep remorse will make anyone forgive you. Just don't be philosophical. Never say "These things happen" or "You shouldn't have loaned it to me if you loved it so much." That'll be the end of the blazer and the friendship.

4. She can't stay mad forever. And if she does, what kind of friend was she anyhow?

5. Let's hope you followed the cardinal rule: Never borrow what you can't afford to replace.

Host a Dinner Party? You're Joking.

I'm no Martha Stewart. I mean, I thought a canapé was what hangs over a walkway to keep you dry. Now I'm entertaining people who are used to five-course dinners—and olives don't even count. Can I become an overnight bon vivant?

PB4: The bonniest.

1. Dinner parties are more about looks than food. If the lights are low, the flowers are pretty, and the wineglasses are full, you could impress them with frozen pot pies.
2. Hey, it's a free meal for your guests. And they're in it for the conversation and laughs, anyway. So who cares if the pasta's tough?

3. Besides, if you put ten adults in a room, serve them food and drink, and they can't make their own good time, it's their fault, not yours.

4. Did you ever see those dinner party spreads in magazines? They're not stuffing their guests with elaborate courses as much as they're showing off their antique lace napkins. If you can't do either, just dim the lights some more and open another bottle of wine.

5. My first fancy dinner party was a mess. All the fuses blew, leaving us in the dark with an undercooked roast that I hacked up by flashlight, and a key lime pie that melted in a warm refrigerator. But we had a wonderful time. Which either proves that it's the company and not the food that matters, or that disasters bring out the best in people. So play it safe. Invite delightful people *and* overload your circuits.

Going Gray!

W hat's next, Social Security? Gas-X?
Trifocals?

PB4: At least you'll have money, good
digestion, and sight. Look at the bright side.

1. Sure, those grays are a shock at first, but
   they're hardly in a class with failing eye-
   sight and hearing. In the outfit of life, hair
   is just an accessory, and accessories are
   easy to change.
2. Gray isn't about age. My grandmother
   was a natural brunette until she was sev-
   enty. My friend was completely gray by
   twenty. No one ever mistook them for
   each other.
3. Some people say they earned every gray
   hair on their head, and are proud of it.
   I've never understood what that meant,
   but I like the attitude.

4. Gray hair can be elegant and distinguished. The beauty is, if you decide it's not, it can be brown again in less than an hour.

5. In the list of signs of aging, going gray barely even ranks. Disease, memory loss, back humps—they're the ones you want to avoid.

Addicted to Makeup

W hen I'm not buying makeup, I'm
thinking about buying it. Do I need help?

PB9: Only if your blush is too bright.

1. Everyone needs a hobby, and makeup is
   perfect. It's year-round, open to the
   public, and doesn't require special
   shoes.
2. Who doesn't want to look like Isabella
   Rossellini? If plunking down fourteen
   bucks gives you that hope, even for a
   minute, it's worth it.
3. Of course you have to buy that new red
   lipstick, even if you have fifteen like it at
   home. One shade can mean the difference
   between frump and funk.

4. Look at it as culture. Makeup gives you the satisfaction of being an artist, without the expense of lessons and canvas.

5. You can express yourself by having your chest tattooed and your lip pierced—or by trying a new eyeliner. You tell me which is better.

Obsessed with Wrinkles

W hose face is this, anyway? I'm sagging, wrinkling, and drooping—and the worst is yet to come! I just can't accept the aging process.

PB4: Get in line, honey.

1. Come on. How many women *choose* to look older? Your feelings are as natural as enlarged pores. Don't get down on yourself for having either one.
2. Okay, so you spent a month's salary on skin care products. Hey, if they make you look younger for an hour, it's money well spent.
3. Just because *you* think a 747 could land in the lines around your mouth, it doesn't mean the rest of the world does. Put down the magnifying mirror and dim the bathroom lights. Why look for trouble?

4. No matter how good anybody looks, she's going to get old. In thirty years, even Cindy Crawford won't look like Cindy Crawford. And if that doesn't make you feel better, I don't know what will.

5. Let's face it: It isn't fun or easy to get older. And if thinking positive doesn't help, try drawing a mustache on Julia Roberts's picture. You'll be surprised how good that feels.

I Created a
Decorating Disaster

I spent a fortune, and it still looks like a Before picture. What do I do with a room that screams BAD TASTE?

PBQ: Live with it like everyone else does.

1. You've been looking at too many magazines. If you want perfect, you might consider moving in with Martha Stewart.

2. Who wants a place that looks "decorated"? It's much more interesting to go for a mix—even if it is a mix of bad and worse.

3. Your place probably looks better than you think. Go out, and come back in with a fresh eye. If that doesn't work, go out and come in with sunglasses.

4. Just think of all the rich people who pay interior designers a fortune and then get a place that's awful. Look how much money you saved by doing it yourself.

5. Hey, you didn't tattoo a map of Texas on your chest or give all your money to a cult. You just bought some furniture. Hardly irrevocable.

Parent

Traps

I'm Having a Baby

If I'm so happy, why am I so panicked? I hate to admit it, but the delivery is already scaring me, and it's months away. Is this normal?

PB4: Normal as nausea.

1. You're gaining weight, getting kicked in the abdomen, and about to deliver a bundle roughly the size of a large roast. Of course you're scared. Don't get down on yourself for it.
2. The obvious reassurance is the fact that millions of women have had babies and have gotten through it just fine. Then they willingly repeated the experience. That's more than you can say for some dates you've had.

3. Think of the weakest woman you know who has had a baby. Come on, if she made it, you can have that kid and write the birth announcements at the same time.

4. Unlike allergies or pockmarks, labor and delivery are only temporary. You can certainly stand something that takes less time than a round trip to London.

5. Think of all the hours you've spent in pain with no more to show for it than a pasty complexion. Then think of what you'll get for a few hours of pain this time. It sure beats the stomach flu, and at least you know it's coming.

6. Eighteen years from now, when it's two in the morning and you're waiting to hear the car in the driveway, you'll wish you could go back to the joys of delivery.

Off to School. Already?

Kindergarten starts in a month. She's excited, proud, and terrified. So am I. Can I do something to make this go smoothly for all of us?

PBJ: Smooth as paste.

1. You'll want to tell her all kinds of positive things about school. Just don't go too far and make it sound like Disney World, or your credibility will be shot by naptime.
2. Don't feel awful if, despite your preparation, she dissolves in tears when she gets there. It just shows that she can't be fooled by colorful toys and a grinning teacher. She knows this is just the beginning.

3. Don't feel awful if, despite your preparation, *you* dissolve in tears when you get there. You really know this is just the beginning.

4. Remember that her future doesn't hinge on her performance in kindergarten. In fact, the world is filled with stories about megasuccesses who were written off by their grammar school teachers. So don't get too worked up over daily ups and downs.

5. Though it's tempting, try not to be the prosecutor cross-examining the witness when she comes home from school. After all, do you want to take the stand when you come home from work? Respect her need to decompress. Chances are, you'll eventually hear who threw up, who got yelled at, and who ate paste.

My Baby's Growing Up

Who's this big person living in my house? Yesterday I was the center of her world. Today I'm not even on the radar screen. Have I lost her?

PB4: Hardly.

1. Until she's doing her own laundry and buying her own groceries, she's not gone. She's just out of the house for a few hours a day. Look at it as a chance to switch from *Barney* to *Oprah*.
2. It's not as if one day it's fifth grade and the next day it's singles bars. In the great race of life, she's barely left the starting line.
3. Your job just keeps getting better. You go from bottles to bag lunches. From cradles to carpools. From Disney tapes to CDs with body-part names. And you thought she needed you before?

4. Even if she is preoccupied with her friends, does she call *them* when she gets a stomachache or has a nightmare? You're still the real security she needs.
5. Maybe at her wedding you can feel like your baby's gone. But for now, she's all yours.

Rejection Pains

My daughter feels awful because she didn't get a part in the school play. What can I tell her?

PB4: Plenty. And that goes for any other rejection that comes along, too.

1. Tell her lots of gorgeous, talented people have been in the same boat. Katharine Hepburn, Elizabeth Taylor, Meryl Streep, and Meg Ryan didn't get parts in their school plays either. (Okay, we don't know that, but wouldn't that make *you* feel better?)

2. When you were a kid, did you ever want to hear "There's always next year?" Neither does she.

3. Ditto for "It's not the end of the world." Of course it is, for her. Bite your tongue if you feel the urge.

4. Try mentioning all her other accomplishments. If she doesn't want to hear about them, she'll let you know. But who doesn't?

5. The way people get picked for things isn't always fair. Tell her about the time you were passed over for something you really wanted. If you have to make up a story, make it up. That's your job.

6. There's always ice cream. Shallow, but effective.

Home Runs
Aren't Everything

You can pick my kid out of any team. The one watching birds in the outfield while the ball flies by. The one hitting the volleyball under the net. The one who always strikes out, especially in the ninth. Is there anything I can say to make things better?

PBQ: Always. Tell your athlete this:

1. The bottom line is, it's a game. Lives don't hang in the balance. The future isn't in jeopardy. (Maybe that won't soothe every bad feeling, but it can sure take the edge off.)
2. Lots of star athletes weren't stars when they were young. They *became* good with practice and desire. Nothing is out of reach because it didn't go well today.

3. No one can be good at everything. Even Jordan wasn't great at baseball. So what if you miss a ball? Can Frank Thomas play Nintendo like you can?

4. You know, in 1986 Bill Buckner let Mookie Wilson's ground ball skip right through his legs. That blew it for his team—and catapulted the Mets to the World Championship. And he did it on national television. And survived.

5. No matter how bad the game is, the sun will still rise tomorrow, real friends will still be friends, and the world will most definitely forget there ever was a game.

Happy
Birthday
(Really!)

Turning Thirty

I feel so old. I'm past my prime, and I haven't accomplished anything yet.

PB9: Prime? You must be kidding.

1. You're on top of the world. Finished with school, but a good twenty years away from facelifts. Prime isn't even around the corner.
2. This is when the good stuff starts. Careers, meaningful relationships, families, travel. Didn't you ever watch *thirtysomething*?
3. Men reach their sexual peak by twenty. The good news is that you haven't even begun to sizzle.

4. Were your twenties really so great? Remember all those bad decisions, crummy jobs, and lousy dates? This decade is when you hit your stride—smarter, savvier, and a whole lot more fun.

5. Hey, if it really bothers you, look at it this way: At least you're not forty.

Turning Forty

I remember my mother's fortieth birthday. I thought she was ancient. Now *I'm* there, and I can't stand it!

PB4: Of course you can.

1. Sure, the number's a little scary. But forty isn't what it used to be. Some women start having kids at forty. Some start whole new careers. And some finally find the right shade of foundation. That's worth it right there.
2. You thought things were good before? With the wisdom and experience you've got now, they'll only get better.
3. You thought things were bad before? With the perspective and confidence you've got now, they'll only get better.

4. Give or take a few child prodigies, most great people just start getting good at forty. Think about all the writers, painters, actors, and executives you read about. They're not kids. They're not wet behind the ears. And they're not whining about their age, either.

5. The beauty of forty is that you've got nothing to prove. You can wear comfortable shoes and feel fine about it. That alone is worth another birthday.

6. Hey, if it really bothers you, look at it this way: At least you're not fifty.

Turning Fifty

Whoa! Grandmothers are fifty, not me. There must be some mistake!

PBQ: The only mistake is not enjoying it.

1. Sure, it's upsetting at first. But so was the Sonny and Cher breakup. You get used to these things.

2. If you thought you had nothing to prove at forty, you've really got nothing to prove now. Do the job you want, wear the clothes you want, take the trips you want. You don't think that sounds good?

3. My mother used to say, "I look in the mirror and see a fifty-year-old, but inside I'm twenty-five." If you can do that, you'll have the best of all worlds.

4. Okay, so your sight's not as good as it used to be. Okay, so your face isn't as high on your neck as it used to be. So what? It really is what's inside that counts, no matter what the twenty-year-old at the cosmetics counter tells you.

5. Hey, if it really bothers you, look at it this way: At least you're still kicking.

Friends
Forever

The Long Haul

Sure, I've got friends. But what about twenty or thirty years from now? I like to think we'll still be comforting each other and laughing together even then. Am I deluding myself?

PB9: No, just planning ahead.

1. Really good friends stick together. For life. So rest assured that you'll be laughing just as hard over your early bird dinners years from now as you are over your lattes today.
2. Really good friends stay for the triumphs and the tragedies. So rest assured that you won't be alone, no matter what happens.
3. Really good friends grow old together, and they keep telling each other that they haven't changed a bit. That alone makes them worth hanging on to.

4. If you don't think friendships last, go to a coffee shop some morning at seven. You're bound to see at least one table of pals who have been laughing over coffee and fighting over the check for the past thirty years. Doesn't that give you hope?

5. Jobs come and go, sometimes husbands come and go, and kids grow up. But your friends are the constant you can count on—for the long haul.